Nonsuch:
Pearl of
the Realm

by Lalage Lister

"a sumptuous House called Nonesuche . . . is
nowe evident to be beholden, of all strangers
and others, for the honour of this Realme, as
a pearle thereof.

from the *Life of Arundel*, c.1580

Sutton
Leisure Services

ACKNOWLEDGEMENTS

I would like to express my grateful thanks to Professor Martin Biddle, Director of the excavation of Nonsuch, for his kindness in reading and correcting this adaptation of John Dent's *The Quest for Nonsuch*. Thanks are also due to Jane Jenkins, George Jenkinson, Valary Murphy and to members of the Heritage Section at Sutton Leisure Services – June Broughton, Douglas Cluett and Alison Kearns.

ILLUSTRATIONS ACKNOWLEDGEMENTS

Photographs and illustrations were supplied or are reproduced by kind permission of the following. The pictures on pages 8, 77 and 79 are reproduced by gracious permission of H.M. the Queen; on page 63 by permission of Viscount de L'Isle from his private collection and on page 65 by kind permission of His Grace the Duke of Norfolk. The Trustees of the will of the 8th Earl of Berkeley, deceased: 81; Martin Biddle: 103; J.A. Brancher: 102; British Library: 32, 66, 97; The Trustees of the British Museum: 36; Conway Library, Courtauld Institute of Art: 19, 20, 21; Crown copyright, P.R.O. (ref. E36/277): border on prologue and all chapter heads; Estate of the late John Dent: 92; The Devonshire Collection, Chatsworth. Reproduced by permission of the Chatsworth Settlement Trustees: 76; English Heritage: 40, 99; The Fitzwilliam Museum, Cambridge: *cover*, 23, 30; The Folger Shakespeare Library, Washington, D.C.: 59; J.M.I. Griffiths: 95; N.A. Griffiths/Museum of London: 43; Istituto Geografico de Agostini, SpA, Italy: 38, 86, 87; George Jenkinson FRPS: 22, 104-106; Charles Lister: 42; Louvre, Paris: 54; Major J. More-Molyneux OBE, DL: 56; Museo di Capodimonte, Naples: 18; National Gallery of Ireland: 63; National Portrait Gallery: 69, 84, 88; E. Perera: 67; Lord Saye and Sele: 56; Board of Trustees of the Victoria and Albert Museum: 10, 57; Mrs C.F. Winmill: 90.

First published 1992 by
London Borough of Sutton Leisure Services
The Old Court House
Throwley Way, Sutton, SM1 4AF

© Text: Lalage Lister

ISBN: 0 907335 26 8

Designed by Ed Perera, PAD Design

Printed in Great Britain
by Drogher Press Ltd, Dorset

FOREWORD

I first saw a reproduction of Hoefnagel's engraving of Nonsuch as a schoolboy at Merchant Taylors', sometime in 1955, when making notes on Henry VIII's palaces. Nonsuch, I read, had vanished. In that moment I knew I wanted to dig it up, to find out what it had really been like.

Three years later in May 1958 I got to the site for the first time, walked right across it, missed it, and looked for the palace up the slope beyond to the south. Within a few months I learnt that John Dent, the Borough Librarian of Epsom and Ewell, had been following the same trail with more success. With the help of his Assistant Librarian, Jennet Griffiths, he had succeeded in drawing up a hypothetical plan of the palace and in locating it on the ground to within a few feet.

The story of what happened next, of the heroic excavation of the palace in the long dry summer of 1959, and of the banqueting house the next year, was told by John Dent in *The Quest for Nonsuch*, first published in 1962. The enduring popularity of *The Quest* is a tribute both to John Dent's scholarship and to his engaging enthusiasm, which brought the palace alive again for many people, and which was the quality in him I best recall and cherish. What, in his modesty, *The Quest* does not reveal is John Dent's immense personal contribution to the recovery of Nonsuch. Without his organising skill and financial acumen the funds to complete the excavation could never have been raised – in the form of contributions from some 60,000 visitors to the site during the twelve weeks of the excavation.

During these weeks I first came to know his family: his wife Anna, and his son and daughters. No one could be better qualified by her long association with the idea of Nonsuch to write this book for the general reader than John Dent's daughter Lalage. It is delightful that she should have wanted to take it on. For all who have felt the lure of Nonsuch, this book will be an enduring pleasure.

Martin Biddle
October 1991

Hertford College,
Oxford

3

CONTENTS

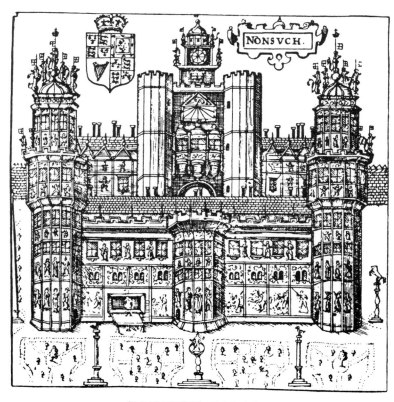

NONSUCH PALACE

FROM THE SOUTH-EAST, FROM SPEED'S MAP OF SURREY, 1610

Border

Border from *Indenture* between Elizabeth I and Dean and Canons of St. George's Chapel Windsor, 30 August 1559 Public Record Office

Tail pieces

Slate guilloche
Stucco cherub
Motifs from embroidery design by Thomas Trevelyon

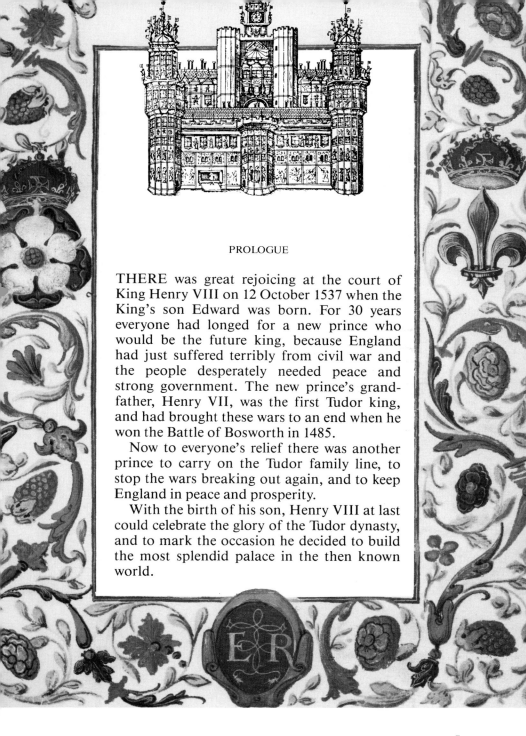

PROLOGUE

THERE was great rejoicing at the court of King Henry VIII on 12 October 1537 when the King's son Edward was born. For 30 years everyone had longed for a new prince who would be the future king, because England had just suffered terribly from civil war and the people desperately needed peace and strong government. The new prince's grandfather, Henry VII, was the first Tudor king, and had brought these wars to an end when he won the Battle of Bosworth in 1485.

Now to everyone's relief there was another prince to carry on the Tudor family line, to stop the wars breaking out again, and to keep England in peace and prosperity.

With the birth of his son, Henry VIII at last could celebrate the glory of the Tudor dynasty, and to mark the occasion he decided to build the most splendid palace in the then known world.

The Tudor Dynasty — Henry VII, its founder in the background, and Henry VIII, who needed a son to carry on the family line.

Hans Holbein (the younger) 1537

He already had 13 other palaces in the London area, but this new one he called 'None Such' because it was to have no equal. It was to outshine even the palace of Fontainebleau near Paris, which Henry's great rival, King Francis I of France, was making stupendous with paintings and carvings and ornate decorations carried out by fashionable Italian artists. Henry had always been anxious to outdo Francis, so he set to work.

He chose a site at Cuddington near London, between Ewell and Cheam, in the middle of good hunting country, for now that he was middle-aged, hunting was his favourite exercise. It was conveniently near to his great palace at Hampton Court, so that he would be able to get back to London easily and quickly along the River Thames.

He chose the spot also for its pure air, coming straight across Epsom Downs, and for its pure water, from local springs. Unfortunately the village of Cuddington was there already, but that was no problem for Henry – he simply had the houses and the church pulled down. He sent for the best foreign craftsmen available, and employing his considerable classical learning and love of the arts he drew up his own schemes for the decorations.

The Gallery of Francis I at Fontainebleau, 1532-1541 – the palace that inspired Henry VIII to build Nonsuch.

Giovanni Battista Rosso

The Seymour Arms incorporating the lions of England and the lilies of France. They were granted to the Seymour family by Henry VIII in gratitude after his third wife Jane Seymour had borne a son to carry on the Tudor dynasty.

Victoria and Albert Museum

The whole centre and point of the palace was to be a huge series of stucco mouldings on the walls of the inner courtyard glorifying Henry himself and his son Edward – their figures were to stand at the focus of the courtyard, among figures of classical gods and heroes and Roman emperors, to emphasise the importance of the Tudors as they looked forward to the future.

The first stone of the palace was laid 453 years ago, six months after the birth of Edward, on the day on which Henry VIII entered the thirtieth year of his reign – 22 April 1538.

A few good reasons for building Nonsuch

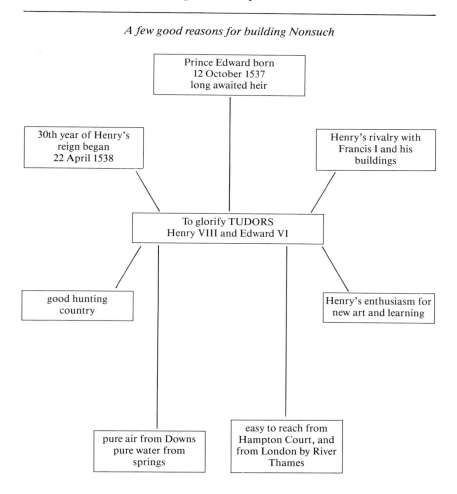

Speed's map of Surrey showing Nonsuch, 1610.

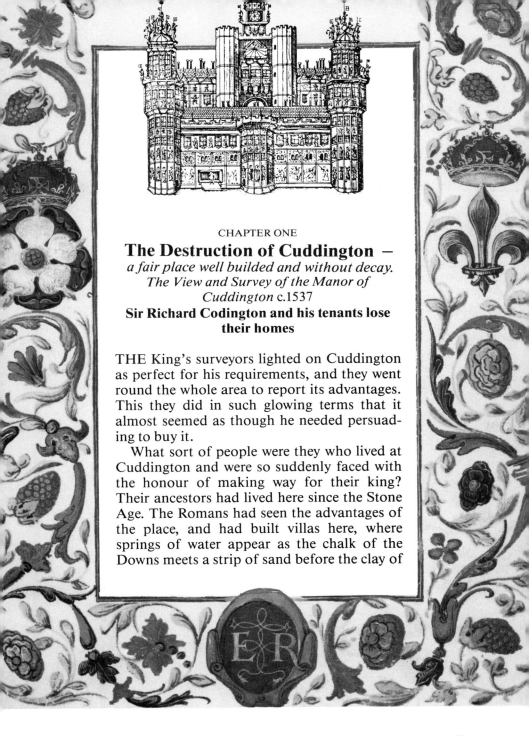

CHAPTER ONE

The Destruction of Cuddington —
a fair place well builded and without decay.
The View and Survey of the Manor of
Cuddington c.1537
Sir Richard Codington and his tenants lose their homes

THE King's surveyors lighted on Cuddington as perfect for his requirements, and they went round the whole area to report its advantages. This they did in such glowing terms that it almost seemed as though he needed persuading to buy it.

What sort of people were they who lived at Cuddington and were so suddenly faced with the honour of making way for their king? Their ancestors had lived here since the Stone Age. The Romans had seen the advantages of the place, and had built villas here, where springs of water appear as the chalk of the Downs meets a strip of sand before the clay of the Thames basin. There was enough water power to drive one mill at Cuddington and several at Ewell, and it was a convenient place to be because the great Roman highway of Stane Street, which ran from Chichester to London Bridge, passed right through.

The most famous person who lived at Cuddington before Henry VIII was the great Walter de Merton, who rose to be Chancellor of England in 1260 and founded Merton College, Oxford. Walter was the Rector of Cuddington, but that didn't stop him being a good business man as well. He bought land round about to give to his sister's family; which became known as the Codington family and Lords of the Manor. These Codingtons flourished, paying rent of a rose a year here, and demanding rent of a pound of wax for the church candle there, until their lands stretched for more than 40 square miles.

There were constant quarrels over the years with their neighbours about grazing-rights – in 1427 one Thomas Codington was awarded a robe of gentleman's livery, with a livery fur, to be given by his neighbour each Christmas to make them 'gode frendes'. One of the last quarrels recorded in the manorial rolls happened in 1509 – an ominous year for the Codingtons, for Henry VIII came to the throne, and soon they would have more serious matters than grazing-rights on their minds. Dispossession was to be the order of the day.

This day finally came in 1537. The Lord of the Manor, Richard Codington, had no say in the matter, but at least the surveyors wrote so highly of the whole estate that the king was inclined to be generous, and gave him in exchange the Priory of Ixworth in Suffolk – not so convenient for hunting or London.

As hunting, the 'royal martyrdom' (as one of the king's secretaries put it), was the reason for the whole enterprise, the surveyors put first things first and stressed that the land was excellent for the purpose. To the south of the manor house the land joined Banstead Downs which, most conveniently, the king already owned. The 40 square miles of country was 'hale and lively' for sheep and coney, pheasant, partridge, fox, hare, badger and 'all kinds of vermin', with good coverts of fir and juniper. There was plenty of arable land and pasture.

When it came to describing the manor-house itself, the surveyors can't have realised that the king was going to pull it down. They stressed that it was 'newly built', and described a typical fifteenth-century manor house, built round three sides of a square, with a great hall, kitchens and servants' quarters, and elegant rooms with good views for the family. Still less can they have understood that the king was actually going to pull down the village church, for they didn't mention that at all.

The griffin fountain which stood in the Inner Court at Nonsuch, over the buried foundations of Cuddington Church. From the Lumley Inventory

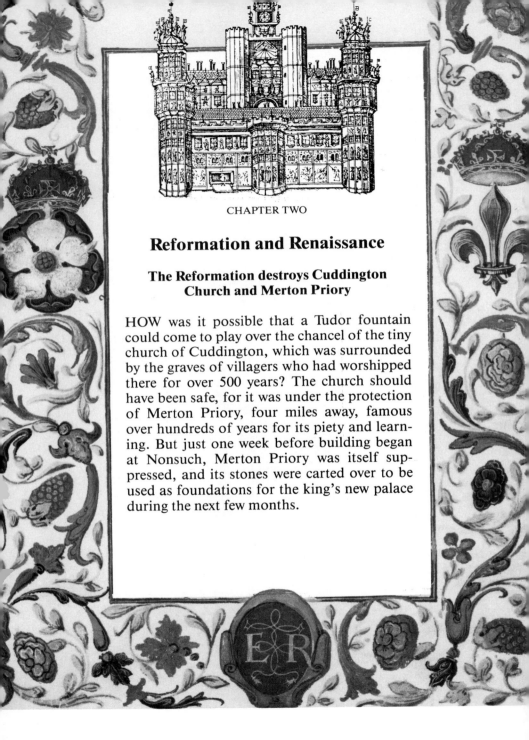

CHAPTER TWO

Reformation and Renaissance

The Reformation destroys Cuddington Church and Merton Priory

HOW was it possible that a Tudor fountain could come to play over the chancel of the tiny church of Cuddington, which was surrounded by the graves of villagers who had worshipped there for over 500 years? The church should have been safe, for it was under the protection of Merton Priory, four miles away, famous over hundreds of years for its piety and learning. But just one week before building began at Nonsuch, Merton Priory was itself suppressed, and its stones were carted over to be used as foundations for the king's new palace during the next few months.

Both Cuddington Church and Merton Priory fell victim to the Reformation — that upheaval in the Church of England which occurred when Henry VIII denied the authority of the Pope, and persuaded Parliament to declare him 'Supreme Head on earth, under God, of the Church of England'. The background to Henry's break with Rome was the climate of new learning and questioning which had been growing up for years, and was encouraging many people to see all that was wrong with the Church and to demand reform.

The immediate cause of the break was what came to be called 'The King's Great Matter' — his wish for a divorce and his need for a son to carry on the Tudor dynasty. His wife, Catherine of Aragon, had no sons living, only a daughter, Mary. So in 1527 Henry decided to divorce Catherine and marry Anne Boleyn. He needed the Pope's permission to do this, but unfortunately for Henry, just at that moment the Pope was a prisoner, and in no position to grant the request — because the man holding him prisoner was none other than Catherine's nephew, the Emperor Charles V.

Henry therefore decided to do without the Pope's permission because he needed a son. With the powers granted by Parliament he was able to suppress Cuddington and Merton and use their stones to build the Palace of Nonsuch to celebrate the birth of that longed-for son. And incidentally, by also suppressing the Priory at Ixworth, in Suffolk, he obtained a convenient manor to pay off Richard Codington.

Pope Clement VII, 1523-34, who refused Henry VIII permission to divorce
Catherine of Aragon.   Sebastiano del Piombo, 1526

The Tomb of Henry VII by Pietro Torrigiano. Renaissance decoration of angels, cherubs and coats of arms in the Tudor Gothic setting of Henry VII's Chapel in Westminster Abbey 1511-18.

Details from the side of the tomb showing figures in a classical roundel of fruit and flowers, and pilasters with decoration of Tudor roses, acanthus leaves and urns in the new Italian fashion.

The Renaissance passion for building

HENRY did as he pleased with the small community of Cuddington — but in doing so he was behaving in every way like a Renaissance prince.

The Renaissance was a period of great turmoil throughout Europe. The rediscovery of the culture of ancient Greece and Rome led people to question the authority of mediaeval institutions. Once the Pope came to be seen not as God's sole representative on earth, but as just another Renaissance prince, new wars of religion broke out, the economy changed, and the whole structure of society was in the melting pot. The balance of power was constantly changing, new people rose to prominence very rapidly, and then tried to build their way into history.

Building was seen as a crucial way of aggrandising new dynasties on their way to the top, and of keeping them there once they had arrived. They wanted to get there in a short time, and stay there a long time. There was no time to be lost.

Henry VIII was in the forefront of fashion when he looked to Italy for artists and craftsmen to build his fabulous Nonsuch. He had already summoned the sculptor Pietro Torrigiano to make his parents' tomb in Westminster Abbey in the new classical style of the Italian Renaissance. Italy was the hot-house of Renaissance style, and because the country was divided into many different states, each with its own ruling family, there were plenty of Italian building schemes going forward. Each state tried to outdo the others in magnificence, because magnificence was power.

This Italian Renaissance style spread through Europe very rapidly after the French invaded Italy in 1497 and took the fashion home with them. They were followed into Italy by the forces of the Emperor Charles V, who included what is now Holland among his domains. The Emperor's forces helped spread the new style still further, so that it reached England via France and Holland.

Eighty years before Henry VIII fell in with this fashion and destroyed Cuddington, the then Pope, Pius II, had set the pattern by destroying his own native village in Italy, because he wanted to build a lasting memorial to his own family, the Piccolomini. He called his new city Pienza, after himself, and built a cathedral and a vast square, with a bishop's palace on one side, and, most importantly, a Piccolomini family palace on the other. Later Popes all had great building schemes, as did, among countless other families

The great gatehouse at Hampton Court. Hampton Court Palace was built by Cardinal Wolsey and vastly enlarged by Henry VIII. The King's Beasts standing on pillars were a favourite Tudor garden decoration, and were to appear again at Nonsuch.

View of Nonsuch from the north-west, 1620. The Outer Gatehouse, the Inner Gatehouse in the centre, the S.W. octagonal tower on the right.

Anthony Watson began his visit here walking along the avenue of trees on the left.

In the Fitzwilliam Museum, Cambridge

in Italy, the Medici in Florence, the Montefeltri in Urbino, the Gonzaga in Mantua and the Sforza family in Milan. Leonardo da Vinci sketched a design for the Sforza castle which was very like the two huge towers which Henry VIII incorporated into Nonsuch.

If Henry needed another example nearer home, he had only to look as far as Hampton Court, where Cardinal Wolsey had built a magnificent palace and lived like a king, although he was actually the son of a butcher. And it was said of Francis I of France, Henry's great rival, that he ordered a new hunting palace as though it were a new suit of clothes. When the kings of France and England met at Calais in 1520, they tried so intensely to outshine each other with their splendour that the occasion was called 'The Field of Cloth of Gold'. They thought nothing of creating a whole new city of tents and pavilions of unparalleled magnificence. The English pavilion was a Tudor mix of mediaeval crenellations and new Italian Renaissance arches and pillars and shell pediments, with statues on the skyline − all in simulated stone and brick. And this was all for a few days' feasting and jousting and chivalric revelry.

Small wonder then that the fate of Cuddington would not concern a Renaissance prince. However, when two years later the Manor of Nonsuch was annexed to the Honour of Hampton Court, to make a huge hunting forest stretching from Walton to Battersea, a clause was added to the Act of Annexation, safeguarding the rights of all tenants. So the four farmers mentioned by the king's surveyors, whose houses, barns and stables were visible from the manor house, and who were 'honest men and tall persons, meet and able to do the King's service', may well have found royal employment. They would certainly have been reimbursed for any crop damage suffered as a result of the king's new building.

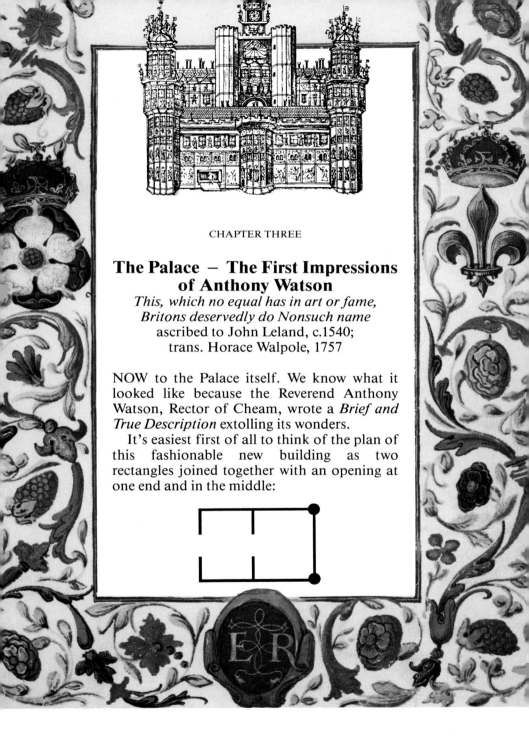

CHAPTER THREE

The Palace — The First Impressions of Anthony Watson

This, which no equal has in art or fame,
Britons deservedly do Nonsuch name
ascribed to John Leland, c.1540;
trans. Horace Walpole, 1757

NOW to the Palace itself. We know what it looked like because the Reverend Anthony Watson, Rector of Cheam, wrote a *Brief and True Description* extolling its wonders.

It's easiest first of all to think of the plan of this fashionable new building as two rectangles joined together with an opening at one end and in the middle:

This was not at all a new plan, for it followed the traditional grouping of two-storey buildings round open-air courtyards – like Hampton Court, many Oxford and Cambridge colleges, and palaces of the time in northern Italy. The layout of the buildings was largely symmetrical, because symmetry was seen as the architectural expression of the harmony which should reign over the well-ordered household within.

Here at Nonsuch our visitor, Anthony Watson, left his horse to be taken to the stables, and walked along a magnificent avenue of elm and walnut which started at the point where the road from London met the road from Hampton Court. This avenue led straight across a bowling green, and then the wide path continued between balustrading and arches to the huge outer gatehouse, which stood in the centre of the facing wall of the outer court.

The whole first impression was of a mediaeval building with a faintly military look. 'This Gatehouse of which I speak, most beautiful in its size and appearance', wrote Anthony Watson, had four octagonal turrets, one at each corner, and rose high above the battlemented stone walls on either side. It was 'adorned with the double support of a stone window' – partly to keep a lookout, but mainly to take advantage of the wonderful views. There were no windows at all along the ground floor, however, as though it was a castle which needed fortification. At Nonsuch these military details of turrets and towers, battlements and windowless walls, were used not for defence but as decorations and symbols of the king's power and magnificence.

Anthony Watson passed through the archway of the outer gatehouse into the outer court. The archway was built so that it echoed any noise five times over – which must have made huge trumpet fanfares sound absolutely tremendous. Up above the arch on the courtyard side was an enormous sundial with the signs of the Zodiac and the figure of Father Time in gold on a blue/green background. The rooms bordering the outer court were for members of the Royal Household. There weren't nearly enough rooms for the full Court, so most retainers had to live in tents which they pitched by the entrance avenue. Several staircases led up to the various suites of rooms. The kitchens were through the courtyard to the left.

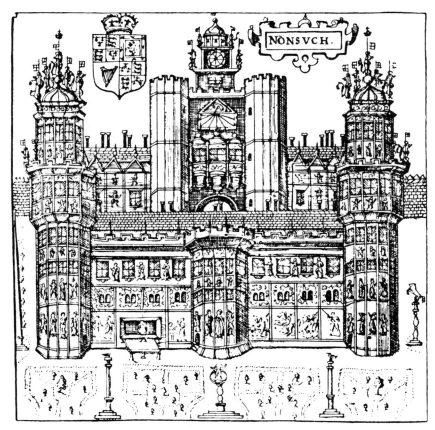

The figures seen by Anthony Watson are shown in this *View of the South Front of Nonsuch* from Speed's Map of Surrey, 1610. The privy garden is seen in the foreground, then the decorated walls and towers of the south front, and over the roof we can see a little of the decoration of the inner court and the inner gatehouse. The figures on the walls were made of stucco duro – that is, very hard plaster stuck wet onto the wall surface and moulded speedily into shape by hand before it dried.

The Inner Court

THIS outer court, quite mediaeval but extremely grand, gave Anthony Watson no clue at all to the splendour in store for him as he walked across the courtyard and up the eight great steps of the inner gatehouse. But as he got to the top of this triumphal flight and gazed through the archway into the inner court he was 'struck senseless' with wonder at the sight before him. For he suddenly found himself surrounded on all four sides by huge figures of gods and goddesses, gleaming white. And there, right in front of him across the court, were the vast figures of King Henry VIII and his son Prince Edward. All these statues were so deeply and excellently moulded that they seemed, he said, to be leaping off the walls towards him. Each one stood in a golden frame that shone so brightly in the sun that it looked as though the Palace were on fire.

Anthony Watson, recovering a little from the shock, saw busts of Roman emperors in majestic progress round the top of the walls; then came the rows of gods and goddesses; and then below these were the Labours of Hercules, all along the King's apartments; and personifications of the liberal arts and virtues along the Queen's side.

At this point, Anthony drew the moral that Henry VIII intended:

> 'Can harm befall the body politic, when its most sagacious King, wielding the sceptre, is protected, on the right, by the arts and virtues and avenging goddesses, on the left by the feats of Hercules and the tender care of the gods: that he may act always in affairs without danger, in leisure with dignity?'

Anthony Watson recognised that Henry VIII, by placing himself and his son up among the gods, was deifying the Tudors, as he needed to do even more now that he had taken over the authority of the Pope. The figures of the inner court were also there to instruct Prince Edward in his duties, forming a kind of memory theatre to remind him of the qualities needed by a Renaissance prince, with mottoes such as 'Know thyself' inscribed at intervals. These images all depended for their power on the idea of a hierarchy in society, a chain of being: that everyone had his place in the chain which stretched from the highest in the land to the lowest. At the top of the human chain was the King. At the top of the animal chain was the lion, the king of beasts. So it was fitting that the figure of Henry VIII enthroned should be resting his foot on a lion. Like went with like, and Prince Edward had to be like them.

Anthony Watson was now standing with his back to the inner gatehouse to gaze at these marvels. This gatehouse, as befitted the entry to the royal apartments, was far more elaborate than the

One of the two huge octagonal towers on the *South Front of the Palace,* from a watercolour by Joris Hoefnagel, 1568. Only the top is visible over the 4m high garden wall. We can see the moulded figures on the walls, and the painted Renaissance pillars.

gatehouse at the main entrance to the palace. The inner gatehouse stood at the centre of the whole palace, and to its emphasis of place was added elaboration of design. It had more graceful crenellations and octagonal towers, and three slender oriel windows on curving corbels. A magnificent sundial above these windows was surmounted by a clock with a delicate cupola. On the corners of little platforms above and below the clock stood statues of the King's Beasts with pennants.

The summit of the palace, its 'chief ornament', the part that could be seen for miles across the countryside, was reached at the far corners of the inner court. Here, two vast octagonal towers, growing wider as they grew higher, rose up to five storeys and dominated the entire building. These towers, like the whole south front, were covered in relief statues, and were especially unusual because they had painted classical columns at each angle – the first time this had been done in England.

Overall, this prestigious palace on which so much artistic brilliance was lavished, was really quite small as palaces go – it was only 137 metres long, and would have fitted into a modern football field.

The outer gatehouse of Nonsuch Palace. Detail from painting in the Fitzwilliam Museum (see p.23).

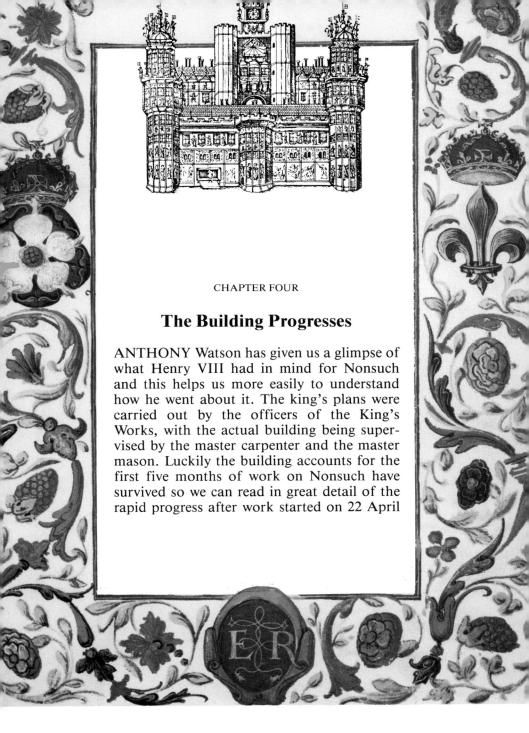

CHAPTER FOUR

The Building Progresses

ANTHONY Watson has given us a glimpse of
what Henry VIII had in mind for Nonsuch
and this helps us more easily to understand
how he went about it. The king's plans were
carried out by the officers of the King's
Works, with the actual building being super-
vised by the master carpenter and the master
mason. Luckily the building accounts for the
first five months of work on Nonsuch have
survived so we can read in great detail of the
rapid progress after work started on 22 April

Carpenters building a timber-framed house.
(From *Ein schön Nützlich Buchlin* by Hieronymus Rodler 1531)

British Museum

1538. Hundreds of tons of Merton Priory stone were brought over to be incorporated in the foundations, with hundreds of tons more of smooth Merton stone used to face the outside walls of the new palace.

We know that the brick kilns on the site not only produced six million bricks, but sometimes damaged the crops nearby — and so four farmers (perhaps the same four the Cuddington surveyors had mentioned as 'honest men and tall persons'?) had to be paid compensation. Raynald Wilkins of Ewell got 7s 6d (now worth (£77.87), Robert Hall also of Ewell 16 shillings (£166.12), and Richard Bray and George Codyngton 25 shillings each (£259.56).

Chalk for mortar was dug locally. Alder saplings were brought in for scaffolding. Wood for the timber frame of the inner court came from forests all over Surrey, Sussex and Kent. The huge trees needed to build the vast octagonal towers at the privy garden end of the inner court were so heavy that the carts pulling them kept breaking down.

The pace was fast and furious: by 10 August, 2,400 small tools and 1,200 stone axes used by the masons had been sent to the smith for sharpening. By 14 September the foundations were finished, and the walls of the inner court had got far enough for some of the window stays to be installed.

Five hundred workmen were gathered, some from as far afield as Wales, and pressed into the king's service. Later on, the records show names from abroad: a German water engineer struggled to get the aqueduct from the spring to flow to the washbasins and fountains; six French clockmakers, French gardeners and a Dutch carver started work. Painters and stucco artists were engaged, and above all there came the prize catch, seized from the clutches of Francis I at Fontainebleau — the stucco artist, carver and painter who designed and worked on the walls of the inner court: Nicholas Bellin of Modena.

CHAPTER FIVE

Nicholas Bellin Comes to Nonsuch

*[This] must needs have been the work of some
celebrated Italian*
John Evelyn: *Diary*, 3 January 1666

NICHOLAS Bellin was virtually on the run
from the anger of Francis I when he left
Fontainebleau and came to England in 1537,
and there was some jealous argument between
the French and English kings about whether
he should be sent back to France or not. Like
many of the artists of the Renaissance he lived
an exciting and occasionally dangerous life.

He had already had to change his name from Nicholas of Modena to Nicholas of Milan, to protect himself when he went to work at Mantua under the great Giulio Romano. When Francis I asked for Giulio to be sent to work at Fontainebleau, Giulio refused to go, and so Nicholas Bellin together with Francesco Primaticcio went instead, and joined Giovanni Battista Rosso, another Italian, there in 1532. The artistic scene round Fontainebleau was enlivened by bitter envious quarrels among artists and patron. Rosso, who designed the great gallery of Francis I which had such influence on Bellin's designs at Nonsuch, committed suicide after a quarrel. There were ambushes, street battles, and constant shouts of fraud.

It seems, though, that Nicholas Bellin left the worst of the infighting behind him when he came to England and entered the service of Henry VIII. Trouble wasn't unknown at Nonsuch: in 1545 the king had to write to his Privy Council complaining that Giles Gering, the overseer of the stucco 'whiteworks' had 'not been here past twice since Christmas last to oversee the workmen under his charge and yet have taken our wages all that time as well as if he had daily continued among them'.

However, Nicholas Bellin was profitably engaged on designing the whiteworks and carving and gilding the slate frames for them between 1541 and 1544, and there is record of his payment for this work. He later worked at Whitehall and Westminster, and as a designer for festival decorations. He apparently felt no need to escape again, for he stayed here for 32 years, until his death. He was buried at St Margaret's, Westminster.

The Inner Court Style

THE style of Nicholas Bellin's designs for the walls of the inner court was the style he had learnt at Mantua and Fontainebleau. He kept in touch with the latest ideas from Fontainebleau and sketches were sent over to him.

Fashionable artists were now no longer concerned with presenting a window on the world, through which the viewer was drawn as though into a natural scene in a picture. The great artists of the earlier Renaissance had perfected that technique, and later artists and patrons wanted something new. The artists at Fontainebleau were now concerned with stunning the viewer with their own artistic skill, and with their patron's power and wealth.

A shield made in Mantua where Nicholas Bellin worked before he went to
Fontainebleau. We can see the kind of surface decoration that was very popular
there − elaborate twisting human figures with decorated surrounds, animal
masks, patterns of flowers and fruit, and a lot of lively movement in the design.

British Museum

They turned for their new style to the relief sculptures of ancient Rome, such as Trajan's column. They made their paintings look as though they were carved on the surface of the canvas, so that the viewer would feel surprised, thrust back and intimidated by them. And when they made relief sculptures, these were very deeply and intricately carved to achieve that same awe and respect from the viewer, felt by Anthony Watson at Nonsuch. The shapes used were not naturalistic either — the human forms were posed in twisting postures, exaggerated and elongated, and surrounded with a wealth of detail of pillars and arches, swags of flowers and fruit, shields, coats of arms and trophies.

It happened that this new decorative style — recently called 'Mannerism' because it is noticeably exaggerated or 'mannered' — settled down very well in England with Tudor Gothic architecture. We have seen that Nonsuch was built with decorative battlements, surface classical pillars and false towers that were there for beauty and not for use. Mannerism and Tudor Gothic were both exaggerated styles with emphasis on vertical lines.

Techniques

Stucco duro — the Whiteworks

THE whiteworks over the outward and inward looking walls of the inner court covered an area of 2055 square metres. Nicholas Bellin used an ancient Roman recipe for the dazzling white stucco. It was made of pulverised burnt chalk and burnt flint mixed with water which dried as hard as stone. It was then whitewashed.

The method used was first to put a wooden backing in the spaces between the timbers of the building. The wet plaster, or stucco, was built up, working very quickly, in layer after layer on these backing boards. Wooden pegs fixed to the boards provided armatures, or supports, to take the weight of the thickest reliefs — some heads and bodies for example were over 23cms deep. All the designs were rapidly built up in the stucco before it hardened.

Hands as well as modelling tools were used to shape the designs, but everything had to be right before the stucco set. Very little could be done to improve the moulded reliefs afterwards, so it was an extremely skilful operation. Besides the figures of gods and heroes on the inward facing walls and stories from Ovid's *Metamorphoses* on the garden walls, the whiteworks were decorated with royal badges and mottoes, garlands of flowers and fruit, horses, rams, cherubs and angels.

Stucco at Mantua worked on by Nicholas Bellin 1527 — showing garlands and
flowing ribbons.   Hall of the Winds, Palazzo del Tè

Stucco at Fontainebleau, 1543, by Francesco Primaticcio in the Mannerist style —
on the surface, twisting forms, elaborate surrounds and loaded with elegance.

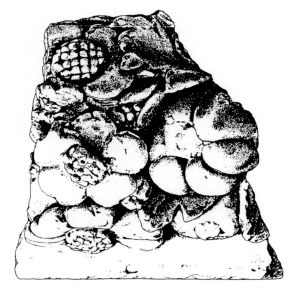

Two fragments of decorated stucco found at Nonsuch, showing Tudor roses and fruit — it should be imagined in a setting like the Primaticcio stucco on page 39.

Drawn by David Honour.

An Elizabethan garden showing a green walk with arcading and pattern of knots.
Drawn by Charles Lister from a painting by Isaac Oliver

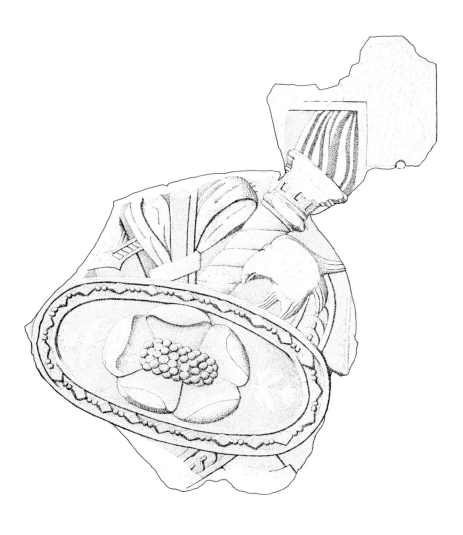

A slate trophy found at Nonsuch with a Tudor rose and a flaming torch.
Drawn by Nicholas Griffiths.

Slate

THE whiteworks were enclosed in frames made from carved and gilded slate attached to the horizontal and vertical timbers of the building. These slate frames were carved in elaborate twisted forms, or guilloches. There were also slate pillars with arabesque patterns cut into them. As with the stucco there were countless decorations of flowers and fruit, Tudor roses, flaming torches, scrolls, crowns, and grotesques – elaborate tendril designs of the kind found in excavations of the Golden House of the Emperor Nero in Rome. The style of carving was similar to the woodcarving at Fontainebleau.

The idea of slate being used to cover timber came from France, but its use on a huge decorative scale was unique to Nonsuch. It was such difficult and exacting work to carve it that Nicholas Bellin kept the job for himself and his 'company' – a small team of six, most of whom were probably French. Many of the pieces of slate had fixing instructions written on the back in French.

CHAPTER SIX

The Gardens — Anthony Watson takes a stroll

A silver spring bursts forth with sparkling waters
Anthony Watson, Rector of Cheam:
Description of Nonsuch, c.1582-1592

NONSUCH Palace was surrounded by 16 acres of fantasy gardens set within the 671 acres of the Little Park. The Little Park joined the Great Park which was stocked with deer 'where the delights of hunting may be enjoyed'.

The Privy Garden

FOR his tour of the gardens, Anthony Watson started in the king's privy garden by the end of the inner court. 'From there, if you turn your gaze to the lofty towers, the turreted walls, the projecting windows, the plaster-work, the excellent statues, you will wonder

The Venus fountain from the privy garden at Nonsuch.

From the Lumley Inventory

whether you are walking in courtyard or garden, for the face of each has the same splendour and majesty.'

The privy garden had symmetrical beds with small plants and patches of colour in patterns called 'knots' as they were designed 'mingled in intricate circles' as though they were embroidered. Among them were small stone animals covered in green creepers. As the queen looked down from the bay window of her bedroom on the first floor she would have seen 'a new paradise', with a fountain of Venus on a small hillock in the centre, surrounded by statues. This was a garden with a hint of the mediaeval, with its high wall and green galleries of trees with seats; but it was laid out on a grander scale, in an Italian Renaissance manner, to emphasise the importance of the Tudor dynasty.

The flowers at Nonsuch were not as varied as those we have today. There is a list of those ordered for Hampton Court that were sent along to Nonsuch − roses, wallflowers, sweet williams, violets and primroses. Anthony Watson noticed also yellow and purple hyacinths, daffodils and lilacs; and herbs growing among the flowers − sweet-smelling savory, thyme 'that gives honey of exceptional flavour', rosemary, hyssop and mint.

Fruit trees were grown not just in the orchard but in the privy garden as well. Along with yew, cypress, bay, holly, oak and elm were apples, pears and cherries. The king sent his chief gardener, a priest named Woolf, to Europe to seek out the latest trees, including the apricot. Another gardener, Robert Harris, was sent to fetch 'out of France a great store of grafts, especially pippins, before which there were no pippins in England'. A M. de Sens sent 200 pear trees from France, and Henry VIII commanded a French garden specialist to be at Nonsuch when they were planted, to make sure they did well.

Carrying on along the king's side of the palace, Anthony Watson came upon a mysterious maze: 'you will enter a tortuous path and fall into the hazardous wiles of a labyrinth, whence even with the aid of Theseus's thread you will scarce be able to extricate yourself'.

The Wilderness
EMERGING at last, he left the privy garden and entered the wilderness, 'which is, in fact, neither wild nor deserted'. This theatrical forest 'is set out with magnificent tree-lined walks . . . At the

Patterns of knots made from small plants and coloured gravels for a formal
garden.   From Gervaise Markham's *Country Farm* 1615

end of the path to the south, the trees have been trimmed to form canopies . . . There are trees for shade and for fruit: almost countless young apple-trees, shrubs, evergreens, ferns, vines. To the north is a widespreading circular plane-tree, its branches supported on posts, so that many people can sit beneath it, talking, listening to the calls of animals and birds, or gazing at the wire-fenced aviary.' There were also spaces enclosed for ball-games.

The Grove of Diana

FLUTE music was playing as Anthony Watson left a stone menagerie of wild animals which 'scarce retaliate even when attacked', and walked from the wilderness to the grove of Diana. Here he found 'Diana herself lurks in the shadows' and he described a statue of Diana, the mythological goddess of hunting. She was shown just as she had turned the unfortunate hunter Acteon into a stag to be devoured by his own hounds, because he had dared to catch sight of her bathing in her forest pool. The statue stood on a fountain fed by a spring. Surrounding rocks formed a grotto, and flowers grew in the spray. This was a symbolic garden with a temple in honour of Queen Elizabeth, for whom poets thought the cult of Diana the Virgin Goddess was particularly appropriate. Early in the next century a bandstand would be built here for concerts.

The Surprise Pyramid

THIS wonderful series of gardens at Nonsuch was made to delight by its beauty, the view, the sweet smell of flowers and herbs, the dappled shady walks, reminders of gods and goddesses, entertainments, and − a surprise. The 'surprise' was the latest Italian Mannerist idea, and Nonsuch's Mannerist trick, a great joke, was an innocent-looking pyramid which deluged the visitor with shutes of water when he unwittingly activated the mechanism by treading on a particular stone − all part of the ploy to make the visitor exclaim in wonder and feel inferior.

The Banqueting House

FOLLOWING Anthony Watson we arrive at the chief place of entertainment in the gardens: 'on a small hill, neighbouring these pleasant places, a most sumptuous Banqueting House was erected'. This was an elaborate garden pavilion, like the temporary festival entertainment pavilions that were the rage, decorated and

The Diana fountain from the grove of Diana at Nonsuch.

From the Lumley Inventory

Elaborate formal gardens surrounded by pleached green alleys of interlaced trees for cool shade. A gateway through a triumphal arch leads to further wanderings in the top scene, while in the lower garden there is a central arbour with seats for resting.   From *Hortus Floridus* by Crispin de Pass 1614

A view of Rosso's Gallery of Francis I at Fontainebleau gives us a hint of the designs at Nonsuch.

made out of branches and flowers, with rose petals on the floor and stars on the ceiling. The Nonsuch banqueting house was rectangular with towers at each corner from which guests could watch the hunting or admire the view. There was a 16 metre wide promenade all round the outside, and the outline this formed was like a fifteenth-century military fort. This promenade was for outdoor musical entertainment in the summer, and light refreshments were taken here after dinner at the palace.

A detail of the Gallery of Francis I at Fontainebleau, showing the elaborately worked carving.

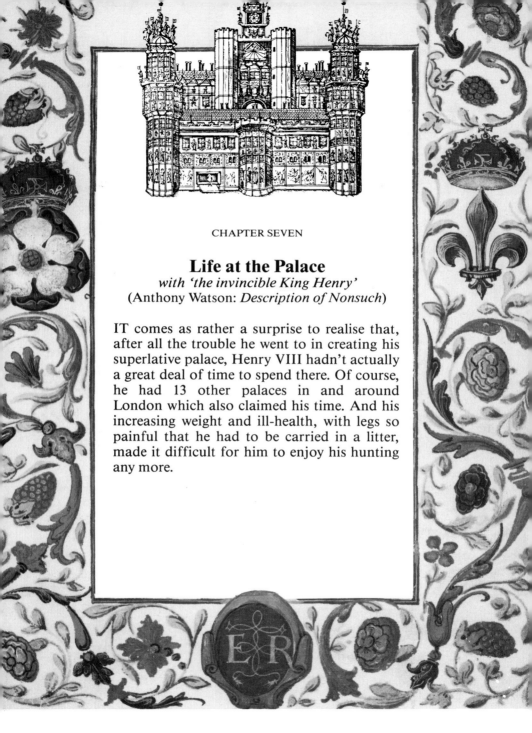

CHAPTER SEVEN

Life at the Palace
with 'the invincible King Henry'
(Anthony Watson: *Description of Nonsuch*)

IT comes as rather a surprise to realise that, after all the trouble he went to in creating his superlative palace, Henry VIII hadn't actually a great deal of time to spend there. Of course, he had 13 other palaces in and around London which also claimed his time. And his increasing weight and ill-health, with legs so painful that he had to be carried in a litter, made it difficult for him to enjoy his hunting any more.

Nicholas Bellin's drawing in the Fontainebleau style. This is the left-hand side of a wall. The design would be reversed for the right-hand side, so the whole wall would be symmetrical. The Louvre Museum

The king was at Nonsuch from 4 to 7 July 1545, and as he held Privy Council meetings there the visit involved all the immense difficulties of the travelling court. A huge train of followers went as well, and the palace had to be granted both extra furnishings by the Keeper of the Wardrobe to cater for the king, and quantities of tents by the Keeper of the King's Tents to accommodate the court. Vast preparations ensued – the country for 12 miles round the palace came under the court's jurisdiction and all the tradesmen in the area had to supply its wants. Enormous amounts of food had to be bought, and the Clerk of the Market made quite sure he got it cheaply.

The job of the Keeper of the Wardrobe was like commanding a military operation. Some furnishings stayed at Nonsuch and some went with the king, and everything had to be checked at the beginning and end of the visit. There was trouble that particular summer because two of the king's huge purple velvet cushions that he sat on in the 'standing' or little shelter to watch the hunting were 'stolen awaie' and never recovered.

The interior walls at Nonsuch were probably plain and covered with tapestries, but we can see what parts of the palace might have looked like from a 'Design for an English Palace' which was sent over from Fontainebleau, and a drawing that Nicholas Bellin made from it. This drawing is for the left half of a wall, so we must imagine it reversed to form the right half to gain an idea of what the finished wall looked like. There is elaborately carved wooden wainscoting, with plaster reliefs above, rather like the stucco designs on the outer walls of the inner court. There is a ceremonial wooden seat in the centre. Henry VIII's name appears, together with the badge of the last of his six wives, Catherine Parr. Another clue to the appearance of the inside of the palace comes from Loseley Park at Guildford, which has some painted panels and woodcarving said to have come from Nonsuch. We know that the Nonsuch windows were leaded, with some stained glass; and we know from a drawing in the Victoria and Albert Museum the sort of fireplaces there were – elaborate white stucco with Mannerist figures and swags of foliage and architectural features. There is a fireplace of this type at Broughton Castle in Oxfordshire.

So we can picture the furnishings against this magnificent background. There are 18 pages in the inventory describing the furniture at Nonsuch, written at the time of Henry VIII's death in 1547.

Painted panels at Loseley Park, Guildford, said to have been taken from Nonsuch.

A fireplace at Broughton Castle, Oxfordshire, in the Nonsuch style.

We read of tapestries, bed-curtains and 'window pieces' in crimson velvet, and in yellow and white satin, all embroidered with classical motifs. Carpets were made of silk and of gold, of tapestry worked with the king's arms and the garter, and of satin, embroidered and painted. There were mirrors, chess-tables, chairs and stools of all descriptions, two small altars for private devotion, and vestments for the chapel.

The king's own four-poster bed was enormous, and with its curtains drawn made a little room which gave warmth and privacy in the bustling open life of the palace. It was described as:

'One bedstead gilt with gold and silver and painted with
light blue, being in length 9' and in breadth 8'7½";
the ceiler [top], tester [back], six small valances and

The elaborately-carved Great Bed of Ware was originally painted in bright colours, and gives a clue to the magnificence of Henry VIII's bed described at Nonsuch.

Victoria and Albert Museum

57

bases made of panels of crimson and gold tissue, purple velvet and crimson velvet embroidered with the King's arms and badges crowned:
with a bed, a bolster and two pillows of fustian filled with down; four quilts of linen filled with wool;
a counterpane 10′ wide and 13′6″ long, made of panels of russet and yellow silk, quilted, lozenged with cord of Venice gold, bordered with embroidery of white cloth of silver, fringed with Venice gold and silver and lined with white fustian.'

This luxurious bed had a very strict security ritual associated with it, which was formulated by Cardinal Wolsey for Henry's visits to Hampton Court. The Gentlemen and Grooms of the King's Privy Chamber had to get up in the morning at six o'clock, light the fire and sweep and clean the room. Then they had to fetch the king's doublet, hose and shoes, and dress him reverently.

Afterwards, when it was time to make the bed, four Yeomen of the Bedchamber stood at either side of the bed, with a groom at the foot, and a gentleman usher holding a torch and giving the orders.

First, the straw mattress was prodded with daggers to find any hidden weapons; then a feather bed was put on top, and a yeoman tumbled all over that looking for more weapons. Then the eight yeomen had to pick up the first sheet, each man holding the edge, and lower it on to the bed very carefully, so that each part touched the mattress at the same time. When the yeomen's hands touched the pillows, they had to kiss each pillow in case they had poisoned it. When at long last the bed was finished, it was guarded by a page until the king retired.

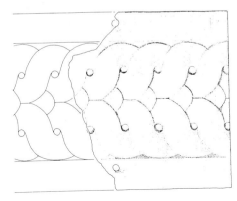

A pattern for embroidery in the style of the Nonsuch hangings, from *Miscellany* by Thomas Trevelyon 1608.

The Folgar Shakespeare Library, Washington D.C.

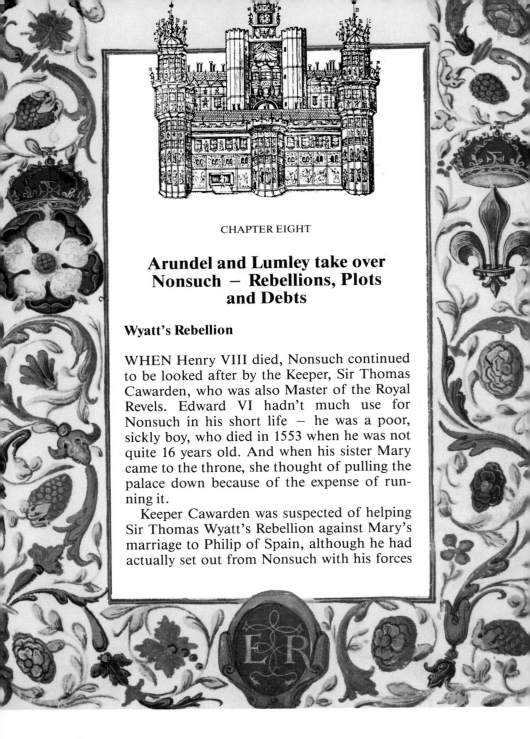

CHAPTER EIGHT

Arundel and Lumley take over Nonsuch — Rebellions, Plots and Debts

Wyatt's Rebellion

WHEN Henry VIII died, Nonsuch continued to be looked after by the Keeper, Sir Thomas Cawarden, who was also Master of the Royal Revels. Edward VI hadn't much use for Nonsuch in his short life — he was a poor, sickly boy, who died in 1553 when he was not quite 16 years old. And when his sister Mary came to the throne, she thought of pulling the palace down because of the expense of running it.

Keeper Cawarden was suspected of helping Sir Thomas Wyatt's Rebellion against Mary's marriage to Philip of Spain, although he had actually set out from Nonsuch with his forces to fight for Mary. Though Cawarden managed to convince the Council of his innocence, his 17 cartloads of cannon, small weapons and armour were confiscated, and only four were returned to him, to keep him loyal. However, Mary obviously thought he wasn't trustworthy, and she sold Nonsuch to the Earl of Arundel as a reward because he had helped her to gain the throne by foiling the plot to make Lady Jane Grey queen on Edward's death in 1553.

When I was fair and young and favour graced me
Of many was I sought their mistress for to be.
(from a poem by Queen Elizabeth I)

MARY died in 1558 and Elizabeth I came to the throne; and at Nonsuch Lord Arundel prepared a huge housewarming party in the summer of 1559. The guest of honour was to be the new queen, whom Arundel hoped to marry as his third wife. The Spanish Ambassador wrote to Philip of Spain:

> 'The Earl of Arundel has been going about in high glee for some time and is very smart. He has given jewels worth 2,000 crowns to the women who surround the Queen . . . I was rather disturbed at this for a time, as an Italian merchant, from whom he has borrowed large sums of money, told others here that . . . [Arundel] was to marry the Queen; but I did not lose hope as the Earl is a flighty man of small ability.'

Arundel set about bankrupting himself by completing Nonsuch and its gardens in accordance with Henry VIII's wishes, and making all ready for the reception of the queen on her summer progress. She arrived on Saturday 5 August 1559. According to an account by Henry Machyn, a merchant tailor of London, the following night Arundel provided the most costly entertainment ever seen at Nonsuch. After supper in the palace, there was a banquet in the banqueting house with a masque, and drums and flutes with 'all the music that could be' keeping the festivities going till after midnight.

On the next day, Monday, Elizabeth watched hare-coursing from one of the standings in the park. Later, after a huge supper, the choirboys of St Paul's acted a play. Then followed a vast banquet

By Joris Hoefnagel 1582.

Queen Elizabeth's procession approaches the south front of Nonsuch.

Queen Elizabeth Dancing Penshurst Place, Kent.

Unknown artist, French school c.1580.

with food served on gold dishes, and music from drums and flutes. The visit continued in this vein till the queen left on 10 August, when her careful host presented her with a cupboard full of gold and silver plate.

The Ridolfi Plot

HOWEVER Elizabeth didn't marry Arundel — or anyone else — and, disappointed in his hopes, he began plotting with Catholics at home and abroad to oust her from the throne in favour of Lady Catherine Grey, sister of Lady Jane Grey. When this was discovered the Earl was put under house arrest for a month, but he carried on sending treasonable messages from Nonsuch to the King of Spain. He was plotting again in 1571, this time with an Italian, Ridolfi, to put Mary, Queen of Scots on the throne, and he was again punished by being confined to Nonsuch.

The Florentine Debt

WHEN Arundel died he left Nonsuch to his son-in-law, Lord Lumley, together with huge debts caused by his extravagance, his periods of imprisonment when he was unable to look after his affairs, and the fact that he had most unwisely taken over responsibility for a debt owed by the city of Florence to the queen. Between them, Arundel and Lumley owed £11,000 to the queen (present day value £1,046,870) and £13,000 to other creditors (£1,237,210).

Because these debts were really unpayable, Lumley drew up a huge inventory of all his possessions to see what he could sell. There are drawings in these lists of the garden fountains and statues with which he and Arundel had beautified Nonsuch, and a record of over 250 paintings he kept at the palace. These were by some of the greatest artists of the day — Hans Holbein the Younger, Albrecht Dürer, Hans Eworth, Nicholas Hilliard, and many more. There was also a 'special picture of Christ cast in mould by Raphael'.

The vast Nonsuch library which Lumley and Arundel had built up, the second largest in private hands, was catalogued. But what Lumley really wanted was to raise the money without spoiling his legacy to his heirs — he was extremely proud of his family tree, and was obviously so boring about it that James I commented 'I didna'

Henry Fitzalan, Earl of Arundel, who hoped to make Elizabeth I his third wife. Arundel Castle, Sussex. Unknown artist.

ken Adam's ither nam was Lumley'. He also didn't want to forego his lavish lifestyle, so in 1591 it occurred to him that the ideal solution would be to let the Queen have Nonsuch and all the expense of keeping it up, while he continued to live there as her Keeper.

Elizabeth loved Nonsuch and she was pleased to take it.

Queen Elizabeth hunting — the huntsman offers her a knife to kill the deer. From Turberville's *The Noble Art of Falconrie and Venerie*, 1575.

A detail from an early 17th century courtier's portrait, showing an elaborate Renaissance architectural setting, probably influenced by work at Nonsuch.

Drawn by E. Perera

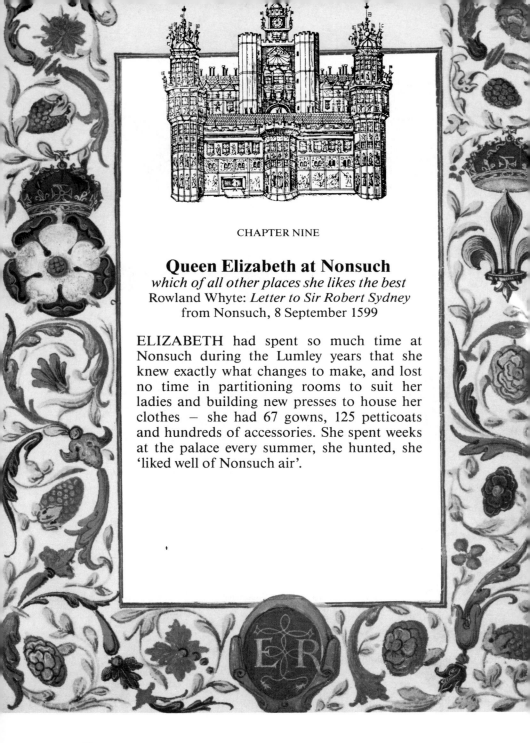

CHAPTER NINE

Queen Elizabeth at Nonsuch
which of all other places she likes the best
Rowland Whyte: *Letter to Sir Robert Sydney*
from Nonsuch, 8 September 1599

ELIZABETH had spent so much time at Nonsuch during the Lumley years that she knew exactly what changes to make, and lost no time in partitioning rooms to suit her ladies and building new presses to house her clothes — she had 67 gowns, 125 petticoats and hundreds of accessories. She spent weeks at the palace every summer, she hunted, she 'liked well of Nonsuch air'.

The 'Ditchley Portrait' of Queen Elizabeth in ceremonial dress, standing on a map of England. Marcus Gheeraerts the Younger c.1592

National Portrait Gallery

The Presence Chamber

ON 23 September 1599 Thomas Platter from Switzerland was privileged to be in the presence chamber at Nonsuch to observe the ceremonies of Matins and Sunday lunch for the queen.

Between 12 and 1 o'clock, men with white staffs came in, followed by 'lords of high standing', and then the queen. Although, Platter says, she was 74 (actually, she was only 66, so she wouldn't have been pleased) – she looked no more than 20, standing erect and regal in a white satin dress embroidered with gold (white for virginity). Her head-dress was a whole bird of paradise, her red hair was studded with jewels. She wore a long necklace of large pearls, and rings on her long gloves.

Elizabeth sat on cushions, flanked on her left by her gentlemen and on her right by her secretary and a 'splendidly arrayed' lady-in-waiting. Then a knight on bended knee offered her books from which she read; after which, the Archbishop of Canterbury, wearing a white surplice, turned to face her and preached his sermon, with responses at the beginning and the end 'just as in the Roman church'. When she'd had enough of the heat and the crowd, Elizabeth signed for the sermon to end, and withdrew to her private room.

And then what to our eyes would be an extraordinary charade took place – the serving of luncheon in the presence chamber to an absent Majesty. But, like the ritual of the making of Henry VIII's bed, it was as much for security as for ceremony, and each detail was strictly, or fairly strictly, adhered to.

First, guards in red tabards embroidered in gold with the royal arms carried in two trestle tables and put them near where the queen had been sitting. Two more guards, carrying maces, next entered and bowed, advanced and bowed, reached the table and bowed. They laid the table and withdrew. Then another two guards, also bowing, put plates on the table and withdrew. A third couple entered in the same way and put carving-knives, bread and salt on the table, which was now considered ready. At last, three gentlemen, two of them carrying maces, and a 'charming' lady-in-waiting, all bowing, came and stood in front of the table to wait for the food.

There then ensued a procession of about 40 guardsmen, each carrying a dish of food which he presented to the lady-in-waiting. She cut off a piece of food for each to taste in case it was poisoned

Robert Devereux, Earl of Essex. William Segar, 1590.
National Gallery of Ireland, Dublin

— but here, Platter noticed, security was slipping, because several of the men didn't bother to eat their morsel. When the carving was finished, wine and beer were brought in and tasted. The dishes of food were offered to the queen in her private apartment: for this very hot day the 'light lunch' included 'some very large joints of beef, and all kinds of game, pasties and tarts'. Dessert followed, accompanied by music from trumpets and shawms. Then the whole ceremony was reversed, and poor old Platter and his friends 'went to a tent before the Palace, and took our luncheon there'.

The Essex Rebellion

FIVE days later there burst upon the court quite the most famous event ever to happen at Nonsuch, and all was in uproar. 'It is a world to be here', wrote one excited onlooker, 'and see the humours of the place'.

This was the Essex Rebellion, and it arose out of rivalry for the queen's attention between the Earl of Essex, her one-time favourite, whom she knew she couldn't trust, and Robert Cecil, Secretary of State and head of diplomacy and espionage, whom she knew she could. Essex was a charismatic patron of the arts and an adventurer who indulged in empty heroic missions abroad, and was not above half-drawing his sword against the queen when she boxed his ears for his impossible behaviour.

He had been sent to Ireland to keep him out of the way, with orders to quell a rebellion there; but he made common cause with the rebels and returned to England to stage his own coup d'état.

His army in fact melted away when he got to London but, nothing daunted, he set off with six companions early on the morning of 28 September 1599 and galloped off to take the queen by surprise at Nonsuch. Overtaken by Lord Grey of Wilton, who was also on his way to Nonsuch to see Cecil, Essex asked Grey to slow down, so that he could be the first to put his story to the queen. But Grey refused and spurred on to warn Cecil that Essex was on his way.

With great bravura and little respect, Essex clattered through the outer court of Nonsuch, and dismounted at the steps leading to the inner court. Dishevelled and muddy, he stormed through the presence chamber and the privy chamber and burst unannounced into the queen's bedroom.

Now it was still only 10 o'clock in the morning, and it takes considerable time to prepare a 'mask of youth' if you are 66 going on 20. So the queen was still without her enamel make-up and without her wig, and she probably looked distinctly unlike the great Gloriana, England's Virgin Queen, whom Platter had marvelled at a few days before. In fact, it's tempting to think that this hugely tactless intrusion was almost Essex's greatest mistake. However, he was sent away to change and the queen granted him a short but gracious intervew at midday.

Later on, when Cecil had told her the true state of affairs, she upbraided Essex for deserting his post in Ireland, confined him to his room, and appointed four members of the Council to ascertain the truth of the rebellion rumours. The next day Essex was kept standing for five hours while he was interrogated by the full Council, and on 2 October he was imprisoned in London. When he was released, after a year, he started plotting and rabble-rousing again, till Cecil managed to get him tried and executed in 1601.

One of the followers who rode to Nonsuch with Essex that autumn day was Elizabeth's godson, her 'boy Jack', Sir John Harrington. Years afterwards in a letter he remembered with horror the interview he had with her in the privy chamber, when she rasped: 'What, did the fool bring you too? Go back to your business!' Furiously she strode up and down, and grabbed his girdle as he knelt before her. 'By God's Son, I am no Queen. That man is above me!' This 'sore hurt' Harrington but, as his parents had been friends of her youth, Elizabeth forgave him for their sake and sent him home. 'I did not stay to be bidden twice; if all the Irish rebels had been at my heels I should not have made better speed, for I did now flee from one whom I both loved and feared too.'

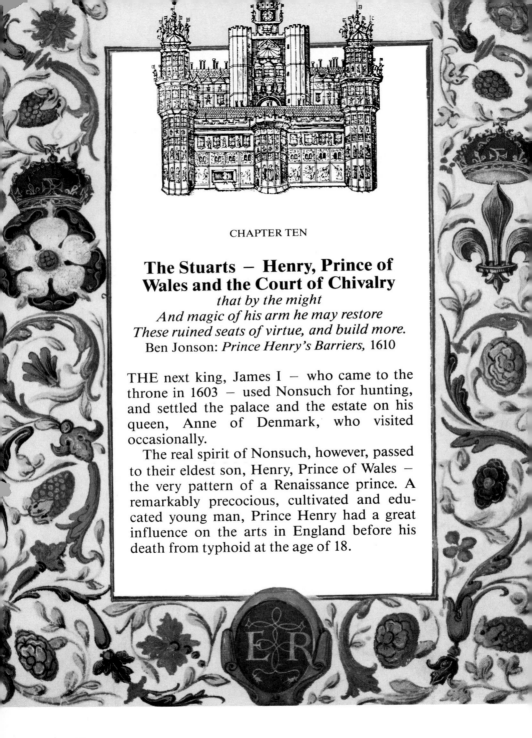

CHAPTER TEN

The Stuarts — Henry, Prince of Wales and the Court of Chivalry

that by the might
And magic of his arm he may restore
These ruined seats of virtue, and build more.
Ben Jonson: *Prince Henry's Barriers,* 1610

THE next king, James I — who came to the throne in 1603 — used Nonsuch for hunting, and settled the palace and the estate on his queen, Anne of Denmark, who visited occasionally.

The real spirit of Nonsuch, however, passed to their eldest son, Henry, Prince of Wales — the very pattern of a Renaissance prince. A remarkably precocious, cultivated and educated young man, Prince Henry had a great influence on the arts in England before his death from typhoid at the age of 18.

The prince established his quarters on the queen's side at Nonsuch and spent many of his childhood summers there. It was at Nonsuch that James Cleland wrote *The Institution of a Young Nobleman,* describing the school of courtesy set up there for the education of Prince Henry and his friends. They were taught all the knightly arts of chivalry, fighting and horsemanship, and all the courtly virtues were encouraged, so that Prince Henry developed into a cult-figure of perfection. As he grew older the prince patronised the arts, the sciences, learning and exploration: he was a diplomat and a connoisseur of a kind hardly known before in England, and certainly not in the royal family.

One of the tutors who had great influence over his development was Lord Lumley, still living at Nonsuch, who fired the prince with his own love of collecting, of Italy and of grand gardens. Lumley's collection of portraits by Holbein inspired Prince Henry to send to Florence for copies of paintings in the Medici collection, and he went far beyond Lumley in collecting paintings as works of art rather than historical records. The prince imported the first Italian bronzes into England, a series by the Mannerist sculptor Giambologna, including a statuette of a horse that his younger brother Charles pressed into his hands to comfort him as he lay dying.

Above all, Prince Henry inherited Lumley's famous Nonsuch library. The nucleus of this collection had belonged to Archbishop Cranmer, who was Archbishop of Canterbury under Henry VIII and Edward VI. It passed to the Earl of Arundel, who built it up to 1,000 volumes, and then to Lumley who enlarged it to 3,000. It was recorded in his catalogue of 1596 under seven headings: Theology; History; Art and Philosophy; Medicine; Cosmography and Geography; Law; and Music. This library, via Prince Henry, became the core of the Royal Library eventually presented to the British Museum by George III, and is now part of the British Library.

One of the favourite court activities was the acting of masques, in which the queen and Prince Henry took part. Just before he was created Prince of Wales, Henry made his first public appearance in a masque called *Prince Henry's Barriers.* He played the part of the hero who rescues Chivalry from disaster and defeat. For this masque Inigo Jones, the Prince's Surveyor, designed scenery showing the classical House of Chivalry collapsed in ruins, with one single building left standing in the centre. This was St George's Portico, from which the hero galloped to save Chivalry; and St George's Portico was a Gothic structure, with Renaissance over-tones — not unlike Nonsuch itself.

St George's Portico — a Gothic building with Renaissance details — standing alone among classical ruins.
Scenery by Inigo Jones for the masque *Prince Henry's Barriers,* 1610.

Henry Stuart, Prince of Wales dressed as a chivalrous knight, with war tents in the background.

Isaac Oliver, c.1612.

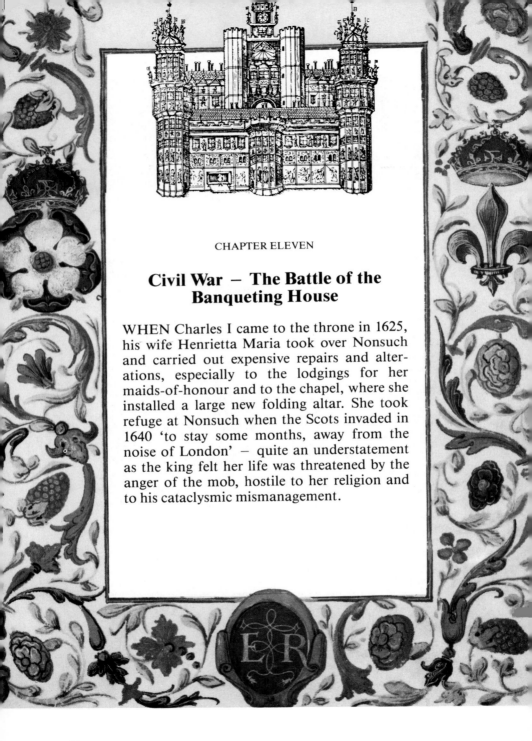

CHAPTER ELEVEN

Civil War — The Battle of the Banqueting House

WHEN Charles I came to the throne in 1625, his wife Henrietta Maria took over Nonsuch and carried out expensive repairs and alterations, especially to the lodgings for her maids-of-honour and to the chapel, where she installed a large new folding altar. She took refuge at Nonsuch when the Scots invaded in 1640 'to stay some months, away from the noise of London' — quite an understatement as the king felt her life was threatened by the anger of the mob, hostile to her religion and to his cataclysmic mismanagement.

King Charles I and Queen Henrietta Maria prepare to go hunting.

Daniel Mytens c.1630-2 at Hampton Court

When the Civil War between King and Parliament broke out, life at Nonsuch continued much as usual — apart from the night when 200 Cavaliers came to stay and were reported to the Parliamentary forces at Kingston by a Nonsuch gardener, whose information was ignored. But when the king was captured and imprisoned, first at the nearby Palace of Oatlands and then at Hampton Court, the Roundheads decided to keep a special watch on all the royal palaces, including Nonsuch, in case of trouble.

At the beginning of July 1648 the king's friends the Earl of Holland, the Duke of Buckingham, Lord Francis Villiers and the Earl of Peterborough assembled their forces at Kingston and waited for reinforcements. When none came, they marched towards Reigate, but were ambushed by the Roundhead Colonel Rich's Regiment of Horse. The Royalists retreated to Nonsuch, where a bloody battle took place near the banqueting house. Many of them were killed, including Lord Francis Villiers, who refused an offer to spare his life, saying that he preferred to die fighting for his king.

On Friday 7 July the Roundheads issued from Nonsuch *A Letter of a Great Victory* claiming Royalist losses of 23 dead, 200 wounded and 100 prisoners, together with the capture of arms, ammunition, stores and plunder. The Roundhead losses were put at only 3 dead and 20 wounded.

The Parliamentary Survey 1650

THE story of Nonsuch as a royal palace now drew to an end. The building stood for another 33 years, but was never again to see the glory that had made it 'the very top of ostentation for show'. The aim of the Parliamentarians was now to sell off everything possible.

A detailed survey, which gives us a great deal of our information on Nonsuch, was drawn up. It betrayed not a little admiration for this royal stronghold — the inner court for instance was described as 'richly adorned and set forth and garnished with variety of statues pictures and other antique forms of excellent art and workmanship and of no small cost'. The palace and the Little Park were sold to Major-General John Lambert, in charge of all the Parliamentary forces in England and Scotland, and the Great Park to Colonel Thomas Pride, one of those who had sentenced Charles I to death.

JAMES PALACE TIME OF CHARLES YEAR BANCROFT

Samuel Pepys visited Nonsuch when it was in decline – as pictured here in this *View of Nonsuch from the North-East* by Hendrick Danckerts, 1660. The garden wall is broken and beginning to crumble, and the pinnacle on the south-west octagonal tower is leaning.

at Berkeley Castle, Gloucestershire

When Charles II returned to Britain in 1660, one of the ships that accompanied him was the *Nonsuch,* built by the son of a ship-builder befriended by James I's son Prince Henry 50 years before.

A detail of Hoefnagel's engraving of the southern front of Nonsuch Palace. The other side of the tower can be seen on the previous page, in the painting by Danckerts.

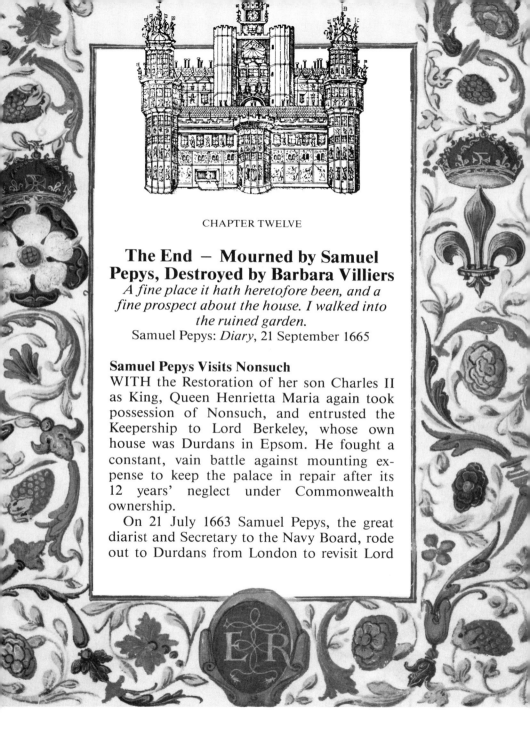

CHAPTER TWELVE

The End — Mourned by Samuel Pepys, Destroyed by Barbara Villiers

A fine place it hath heretofore been, and a fine prospect about the house. I walked into the ruined garden.
Samuel Pepys: *Diary*, 21 September 1665

Samuel Pepys Visits Nonsuch

WITH the Restoration of her son Charles II as King, Queen Henrietta Maria again took possession of Nonsuch, and entrusted the Keepership to Lord Berkeley, whose own house was Durdans in Epsom. He fought a constant, vain battle against mounting expense to keep the palace in repair after its 12 years' neglect under Commonwealth ownership.

On 21 July 1663 Samuel Pepys, the great diarist and Secretary to the Navy Board, rode out to Durdans from London to revisit Lord

Samuel Pepys, lively diarist, man-about-town, and brilliant administrator, visited the Exchequer at Nonsuch in connection with his work for the Navy.
John Hayls 1666, National Portrait Gallery

Berkeley's house 'where I have been very merry when I was a little boy'. On his way home, a mile past Nonsuch, his 'little dogg fell a-running after a flock of sheep feeding on the common', and then got lost. So Pepys arranged to stay the night in Ewell and sent men to look for the dog. While his supper was being got ready Pepys walked over to look at Nonsuch Palace, where he was struck by the sadness of a great house in decline.

The Great Plague and the Great Fire of London

TWO years later Pepys came again to Nonsuch, for in 1665 London was terrified by an outbreak of plague, and a royal proclamation was issued for the removal of the Exchequer to Nonsuch, which had thus sunk to being used as government offices. The same move was made the following year when fire broke out in London. As Pepys was in charge of navy supplies for the war then in progress against Holland he had to pay frequent visits to the Exchequer. On 21 September 1665, when he had to wait at Nonsuch for officials to complete his business, he was first of all 'vexed' but then decided to put his time to good use by touring the palace and the gardens. He saw:

'A great walk of an elm and a walnut set one after another in order, and all the house on the outside filled with figures of stories, and good paintings of Rubens' or Holbeins' doing. And one great thing is that most of the house is covered, I mean the posts, and quarters in the walls, covered with lead, and gilded.'

These paintings are a mystery, for no one else mentions any actual painted pictures on the outside walls of the inner court. But it is possible there were pictures, as there is an example of that kind of decoration that Pepys mentioned on outside walls in Mantua, where Nicholas Bellin worked before he went to Fontainebleau and Nonsuch. There, at the Palazzo del Tè in Mantua, is a garden courtyard, a secret garden, where Giulio Romano designed alternating stucco and painted panels.

Pepys's friend John Evelyn also visited Nonsuch, on 3 January 1666, and commented on the reliefs of the inner court:

'I much admired how they had lasted so well and entire since the time of Henry VIII, exposed as they are to the air, and pity it is that they are not taken out and preserved in some dry place: a gallery would become them.'

Giulio Romano's secret garden at the Palazzo del Te in Mantua, showing alternating panels of stucco and spaces for paintings, as Pepys commented on at Nonsuch. 1525-30

Detail of a stucco panel from the Secret Garden of the Palazzo del Tè, Mantua

(see illustration on previous page)

Barbara Villiers, Countess of Castlemaine, Duchess of Cleveland, and Baroness Nonsuch.

after Sir Peter Lely c.1665-1675, National Portrait Gallery

Barbara Villiers and the Notorious Destruction of Nonsuch

MEANWHILE, Lord Berkeley continued to have money difficulties at Nonsuch, and, treating the place as though it were his own, he pulled down the decaying banqueting house and sold the materials.

Much worse, however, was in store. Queen Henrietta Maria died in 1669, and her son Charles II decided to pay off one of his former mistresses, Barbara Villiers, Duchess of Cleveland, by making Nonsuch over to her. Late one July night in Paris nine years later, Barbara Villiers – now Baroness Nonsuch – gambled away £20,000 (present value £1,062,400) and most of her jewellery in one fell swoop. She had once been very powerful at court, so now that she was absolutely desperate for money she decided to make one more trip back to London to see what she could get out of the king. But Charles II was wise to her, and warned his Commissioners to his Treasury that she was on her way to have a 'bout' with them – and she didn't get her money.

So her thoughts turned to Nonsuch, which she regarded as an expensive white elephant. Its running costs were still enormous and its only value to her lay in the building materials, so she set to work to destroy it. In 1682 Charles II issued a warrant allowing her to pull it down, and she sold the materials to Lord Berkeley, who took some of them to rebuild Durdans. She made £1,800 on the deal – worth £95,616 today.

Nonsuch, once 'evident to be beholden, of all strangers and others, for the honour of this realm, as a pearl thereof', had lasted 142 years.

Remains of the banqueting house at Nonsuch, photographed by Mrs C.F. Winmill in 1960.

EPILOGUE – HOW DO WE KNOW?

The place, and only the place, where that other splendid
Palace of Nonsuch lately stood: a fit subject of reflection
for those who are inclined to moralise on the frailty,
uncertainty and vicissitude of all things.

(John Tolland 1711)

NONSUCH quickly disappeared from sight and, gradually, detailed memory of the building fell out of mind. It was gardened over and farmed over, and in time people completely forgot where exactly it had stood.

So how do we now know so much about that fantastic dream that faded so long ago? How do we set out to discover it?

By treating the hunt like a detective story and following the clues.

In 1957 John Dent, who lived near Nonsuch Park, decided to try to unravel the mystery, and with other experts he began his search. These are some of the areas he investigated.

1 *Folk memories*   Stories about Nonsuch from local people, handed down from one generation to the next.

2 *Existing remains*   The mound containing the banqueting house cellars which has a retaining brick wall still visible above ground.

3 *Local history*   In 1948 Cloudsley Willis published a *Short History of Ewell and Nonsuch.* He described how he had noticed signs of the foundations of a great building while he was inspecting a new sewer-trench dug in Nonsuch Park in 1935. He noticed similar signs in another trench in 1945, and put forward his ideas on the size and shape of the palace.

John Dent plotted the conjectured site on an Ordnance Survey map, and had it

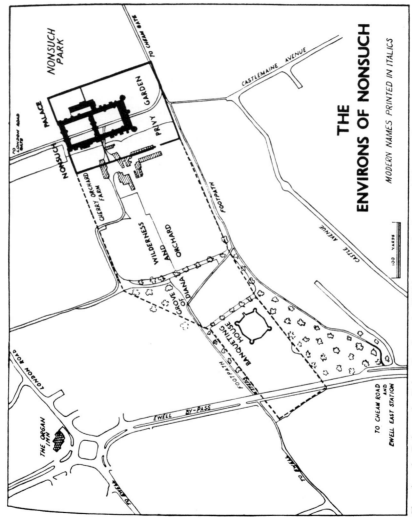

Showing the Palace, the Privy Garden, the Wilderness, the Grove of Diana and the Banqueting House in their present-day setting.

confirmed by aerial photography. He then set out to assemble every mention of Nonsuch he could find to build up as complete a picture as possible.

4   *Fragments in other buildings*

a) *Durdans,* Epsom — Lord Berkeley was said to have taken building materials from Nonsuch to rebuild his own house. Durdans has been rebuilt twice since then, but a search in the oldest part of the cellars revealed some pieces of carved Merton Priory stone which probably came from the Nonsuch foundations.

Design for the tomb of Jane Fitzalan, Lady Lumley, in Cheam Church, showing interiors thought to be of Nonsuch.

From the Lumley Inventory

b) At *Pitt Place,* Epsom, there are two herms — carved human figures used as pillars — said to be from Nonsuch via Durdans (but this is doubtful).

c) At *Thames Ditton* there is a house with panels, door surrounds, and a wooden staircase said to be from Nonsuch (also doubtful).

d) *Loseley Park,* Guildford, has carved wooden panelling and painted canvas panelling said to have come from Nonsuch. The painted panels may be part of Sir Thomas Cawarden's stock of stage scenery, which he kept as Master of the Revels (also doubtful).

e) *Cheam Church* — the tomb of Jane Fitzalan, Lady Lumley, is said to show backgrounds of rooms at Nonsuch.

5 *Commentaries by visitors to Nonsuch*

a) *John Leland* — librarian and antiquary to Henry VIII — *Leland's Itinerary* published 1710 and 1769.

b) *Anthony Watson* — Rector of Cheam — wrote a *Brief and True Description* in the mid 1580s.

c) *William Camden* — *Britannia,* 1586.

d) *Paul Hentzner* — *Travels,* 1598.

e) *Thomas Platter* — *Travels in England,* 1599.

f) *Samuel Pepys* — *Diaries* for 1663, 1665, 1666.

g) *John Evelyn* — *Diary* for 1666.

All these accounts build up a word picture of Nonsuch, which can be filled out with the following four topographical pictures.

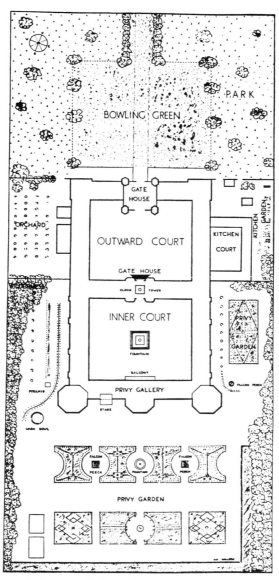

A plan of Nonsuch drawn up before the excavation from information in the Parliamentary Survey 1650, and Cloudsley Willis' *Short History of Ewell and Nonsuch.* Compare with the excavation plan on page 103.

6 *Pictures of
   Nonsuch*

a) *Joris Hoefnagel — South Front of
Nonsuch —* drawing and watercolour
1568; engraving 1582. The watercolour
was discovered in 1963.

b) *John Speed — South Front and Privy
Garden,* with Inner Court and Inner
Gatehouse — a view of Nonsuch in the
corner of Speed's *Map of Surrey,* 1610.

c) Unknown Flemish artist — the
Fitzwilliam Museum oil painting of
Nonsuch Palace, c.1620.

d) *Hendrik Danckerts —* oil painting of
Nonsuch from the North-East, 1660.

Also:

e) *Nicholas Bellin — Drawing for the
decoration of an English Palace* in the
Fontainebleau manner, 1543-1547
(discovered in 1969).

7 *Documents*

a) *Fitznells Cartulary —* mediaeval life at
Cuddington, 1215-1466.

b) *View and Survey* of the Manor of
Cuddington, 1537.

c) *Nonsuch Building Accounts* 22 April
1538 — 14 September 1538.

d) *Palace Wardrobe Inventory —* eighteen
folios on Nonsuch, 1547.

e) *Lumley Inventory,* 1590, and *Library
Catalogue,* 1596.

f) *Parliamentary Survey —* invaluable for
drawing up pre-excavation plan of the
Palace, 1650.

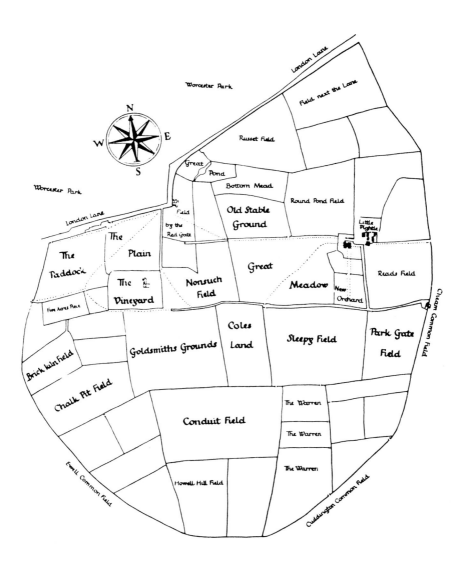

Only fifty years after its destruction, Nonsuch Palace itself wasn't worth a mention in this Survey of the Little Park, drawn up for Joseph Thompson in 1731.

8 *Maps*

a) *Speed,* 1610.

b) *John Ogilby,* 1675, showing site of Nonsuch.

c) *Survey for Joseph Thompson,* 1731, actual site of palace disappeared, shown only as Nonsuchfield.

d) *James Edwards,* 1790, showing site.

Painted glass, found during the excavations at Nonsuch, showing part of the motto *Dieu et mon droit.*

A drawing of a complete panel of stucco duro, based on a reconstruction from fragments found at the foot of the south-west octagonal tower and subsequently pieced together. A similar figure seated on a shield can be seen in the Hoefnagel watercolour on page 29, above the spot where the pieces were discovered.

Reconstruction and drawing by David Honour.

9   *Art History*

a) Compares the unknown (Nonsuch)
with the known (Fontainebleau, Mantua)
to see what the stucco duro whiteworks at
Nonsuch must have looked like
(*researched by Martin Biddle*).

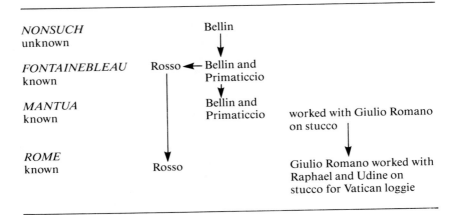

b) We know that slate was used to cover
timber in France, especially in the Loire
valley.

c) We know that Leonardo da Vinci drew a
sketch for the Castello Sforza in Milan,
showing towers like those at Nonsuch.

10   *Excavation*

In 1959 all these clues were brought
together and set in context by the
excavation of Nonsuch, which was led by
Martin Biddle, at that time an
archaeological consultant to the Ministry
of Buildings and Works. It was a very
exciting and nerve-wracking time for the
excavators as they tested their theories
about the exact ground-plan of the palace,

and they were relieved to find as the digging progressed that they had been more or less right in their predictions.

This was the largest dig of its kind ever carried out in a single year in England, and it revealed countless evidence to be slotted into the history of the palace. Though the foundations had to be covered over again at the end of the dig in order to protect them, the work of sorting the material is still going on.

For instance, Cuddington Church with its skeletons was discovered under the inner court. Pieces of pottery, glass, inscriptions and slate, and part of an armillary sphere (perhaps belonging to Henry Stuart, Prince of Wales) came to light.

Fifteen hundred pieces of decorated stucco were found, and from a group at the foot of the south-west octagonal tower it has been possible to reconstruct a whole panel. With guidance from Hoefnagel's watercolour of the south front and the measurements from the 1650 Parliamentary Survey, scholars have enough information to construct a scale model of Nonsuch.

An aerial view of the excavation — the other half of the palace is under the trees.   Photographed by J.A. Brancher in 1959.

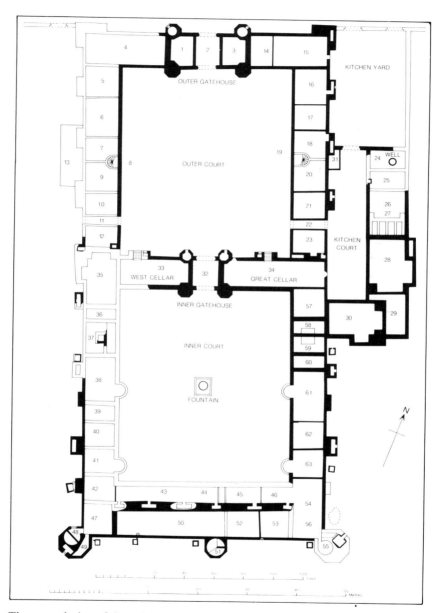

The ground-plan of the palace revealed by the excavation.

A few of the many discoveries at Nonsuch.

Two views of a Bellarmine jug, excavated at Nonsuch Palace, showing its good state of preservation.

Cheam ware jugs and bowl, found at Nonsuch.

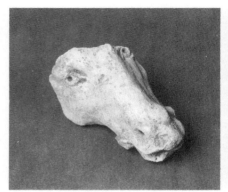

Stucco horse's head

Stucco fragment of fruit

GARTER COAT OF ARMS

Fragments of garter badge in stucco

Portion of stucco crown

WHAT NEXT?

IN spite of the sad destruction of Nonsuch, its story still continues. It had a great influence on many Elizabethan and Jacobean prodigy houses that sprang up, such as Burghley in Lincolnshire, Hatfield in Hertfordshire, Hardwick in Derbyshire, Kirby Hall in Northamptonshire, and countless others.

There are still many pieces of the puzzle missing, which we can all help to look out for.

There are the unsolved mysteries of the whereabouts of the chapel in the palace, Lumley's library, and the stables. It seems that Nonsuch alone among great houses of this period had no great hall – is this because Henry VIII was copying the French system in having no communal meeting place, or is it that there was a hall, but that the signs are not clear to us?

Another problem is that there is no known picture of the banqueting house, but someone may recognise one under another name perhaps, in a museum or a country house. There may also be other pictures of the palace around that are wrongly identified at the moment: the Danckerts picture of Nonsuch from the northeast that hangs in Berkeley Castle, Gloucestershire, was thought until recently to be of St James' Palace; and the picture in the Fitzwilliam Museum, Cambridge, of Nonsuch from the north-west was thought at one time to be of Richmond Palace. The Hoefnagel watercolour version of the south front of Nonsuch, which gives much clearer views of the whiteworks than his two later versions, only came to light by chance in a nursery corridor in a house in Wiltshire.

Apart from all these discoveries, nature is still playing its part in the saga – on the night of the great hurricane of 15 October 1987, one of the trees that blew down in Nonsuch Park revealed a secret it had kept for 300 years. As the roots tore away from the earth, the rainwater soakaway for the privy garden's fountain of Venus emerged.

APPENDIX

NONSUCH TIME – EVENTS DESCRIBED IN THIS ACCOUNT OF THE PALACE

HENRY VIII	Prince Edward born Hampton Court	1537
1509-1547	Merton Priory dissolved	16 April 1538
	Nonsuch started	22 April 1538
	Nicholas Bellin Inner Court	1541-4

EDWARD VI
1547-1553

MARY I 1553-1558	Arundel foiled Lady Jane Grey	1553
	Cranmer's library to Arundel	1553
	Wyatt's Rebellion	1554
	Arundel bought Nonsuch	1556
ELIZABETH I 1558-1603	Arundel hoped to marry Elizabeth	1559
	Florentine Debt	1563
	Ridolfi Plot	1571
	Lumley inherited Nonsuch	1579
	Lumley's Italianate gardens	1580s
	Anthony Watson's account	c.1585
	Lumley Inventory	1590
	Elizabeth took over Nonsuch	1592
	Thomas Platter's account	1599
	Essex rebellion	1599
JAMES I 1603-1625	Prince Henry at Nonsuch	1603-12
	Institution of a Young Nobleman written by James Cleland for the education of Prince Henry	1607
	Nonsuch Library to Prince Henry	1609
CHARLES I 1625-1649	Henrietta Maria − alterations	1627
	Refuge at Nonsuch	1640
	200 Cavaliers at Nonsuch	1642
	Battle at the Banqueting House	1648
	Letter of a Great Victory	1648
COMMONWEALTH 1649-1660	Parliamentary Survey	1650
CHARLES II 1660-1685	Lord Berkeley Keeper	1660
	Pepys visited	1663
	Great Plague ⎱ Exchequer	1665
	Great Fire ⎰ at Nonsuch	1666
	Nonsuch given to Barbara Villiers	1670
	Nonsuch pulled down	1682-3

GLOSSARY

BALUSTRADING:	railing supported by short posts — often of stone
CARTULARY:	collection of documents
CLASSICAL:	belonging to the culture of ancient Greece and Rome
CORBEL:	supporting bracket projecting from a wall
CRENELLATION:	indentation of a parapet
CUPOLA:	small dome
FOLIO:	folded sheet of paper
FUSTIAN:	thick cotton cloth
GOLDEN HOUSE OF EMPEROR NERO:	the Roman Emperor Nero (A.D. 54-68) had a house near the Colosseum; the ruins were excavated in the 1480s, and the painted and stuccoed decorations found there had a great influence on Renaissance art
INVENTORY:	detailed list of goods
KING'S BEASTS:	statues of heraldic animals supporting the royal family arms
LABOURS OF HERCULES:	the superhuman tasks (usually 12, but 16 at Nonsuch) performed by Hercules, the ancient Greek hero of mythology, who was half-god, half-man
LIBERAL ARTS:	the seven branches of learning derived from classical times and studied in the 16th century; they comprised astrology, geometry, music and arithmetic (the quadrivium); rhetoric, dialectic, grammar (the trivium); they were represented at Nonsuch as female figures acompanied by male 'practitioners' — men who were famous for their learning in each subject
LIVERY:	distinctive uniform worn by members of a city company or by servants of one employer
LOGGIA:	open-sided extension to a building
MACE:	club-shaped staff of office
MASQUE:	stylised play with music, elaborate costumes and scenery

OCTAGONAL:	eight-sided
ORIEL WINDOW:	bay window projecting from a building on an upper storey
OVID'S *METAMORPHOSES:*	Ovid, Roman poet (43 B.C.-18 A.D.) wrote 15 books telling stories of the magical transformation of characters in classical mythology
PLEACHED:	intertwined branches or stems forming a fence
PORTICO:	imposing porch attached to a building
PRESENCE CHAMBER:	chief state room at court, where the sovereign presided at ceremonial occasions
PRESS:	large cupboard for clothes
PRIVY CHAMBER:	the sovereign's private suite of rooms at court
PRIVY COUNCIL:	the inner group of the monarch's favoured ministers who carried out royal policy
PRIVY GARDEN:	the sovereign's private garden
PRODIGY HOUSES:	magnificent houses built by courtiers vying with one another for the honour of entertaining the sovereign
SHAWM:	mediaeval musical instrument of the oboe family with a double reed
STAY:	support
STUCCO:	moulded stone made at Nonsuch from pounded burnt chalk and burnt flint mixed with water and dried
TABARD:	short tunic
THESEUS'S THREAD:	Theseus, King of Athens, was a hero of Greek mythology. As a youth he was sent to be sacrificed to the Minotaur (bull-monster) in the labyrinth at Crete. Ariadne gave him a ball of string to unwind as he was led into the labyrinth. He killed the Minotaur and escaped by following the string.
TROPHY:	a group of arms and insignia arranged for display

TUDOR:

English royal dynasty 1485-1603:

Henry VII 1485-1509
|
Henry VIII 1509-1547

Edward VI	Mary I	Elizabeth I
1547-1553	1553-1558	1558-1603

TUDOR GOTHIC:

architectural style — a development of Perpendicular. Basic characteristics in secular buildings:
i) slightly flattened arches
e.g. Great Gatehouse, Hampton Court, 1520
ii) emphasis on height, with tall gatehouses, towers, chimneys, cupolas, lanterns
e.g. Layer Marney Tower, Essex, 1520
Lupton's Tower, Eton College, Berkshire 1520
Clock Tower, St James's Palace, London, 1533
iii) elaborate ceilings
e.g. hammerbeam roof of the Great Hall, Hampton Court, 1533

VIRTUES:

shown as female figures at Nonsuch. Faith, Hope and Charity were the three Theological Virtues; Justice, Prudence, Temperance and Fortitude were the four Cardinal Virtues. At Nonsuch two more virtues, Patience and Humility, were added to bring the total number of arts and virtues up to 16.

WARDROBE:

central office, based at the Tower of London, which bought and administered all furnishings, carriages and harness for the palaces

WHITEWORKS:

whitewashed stucco relief mouldings

SUGGESTED FURTHER READING

For reference on the historical background:

GUY, John: *Tudor England* (Oxford, 1988) O.U.P.
LANDER, J.R.:   *Conflict and Stability in 15c England*
                          (London 3rd ed 1977) Hutchinson
                          University Library
STRONG, Roy: · *Henry, Prince of Wales and England's*
                          Lost Renaissance (London 1986) Thames
                          and Hudson

Nonsuch:

COLVIN, H.M. (ed):   *The History of the King's Works* Vol. iv,
                          1485-1660 pp. 179-205 (London 1982)
DENT, John: *The Quest for Nonsuch* (London 2nd ed
                          1970) Hutchinson
                          Paperback reprint of 2nd ed (1981)
                          (Sutton Leisure Services)

A Nonsuch chest reflects the complex semi-classical design of the palace.